DIATONIC MAJOR AND MINOR SCALES
in Standard Notation and Tablature
by Andrés Segovia

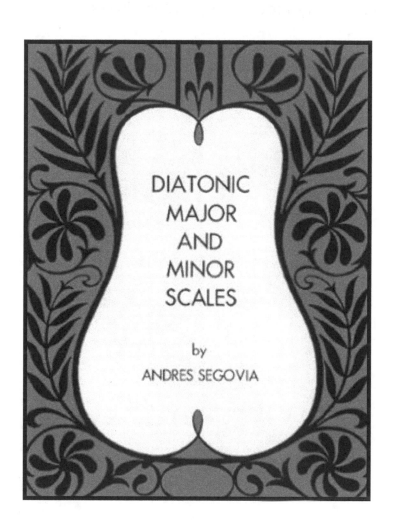

Cover illustration (Segovia at a recital in Brussels, 1932) by Hilda Wiener (1877–1940)

ISBN: 978-1522975823

A. J. Cornell Publications

PREFACE

In order to derive the greatest possible benefit from the following exercises, play them slowly and vigorously at first, more lightly and rapidly later. In one hour of scales may be condensed many hours of arduous exercises which are frequently futile. The practice of scales enables one to solve a greater number of technical problems in a shorter time than any other exercise.

Practice each scale *apoyando* [with rest strokes] seven times as indicated below:

```
i m i m i m i...
m i m i m i m...
a m a m a m a...
m a m a m a m...
i a i a i a i...
a i a i a i a...
i m a m i m a...
```

i = index finger
m = middle finger
a = ring finger

—Andrés Segovia

CONTENTS

C Major

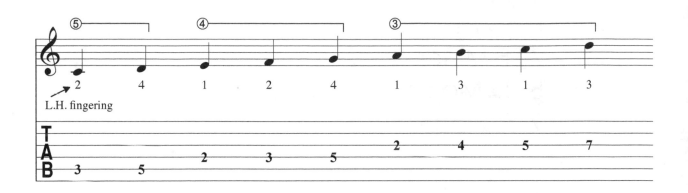

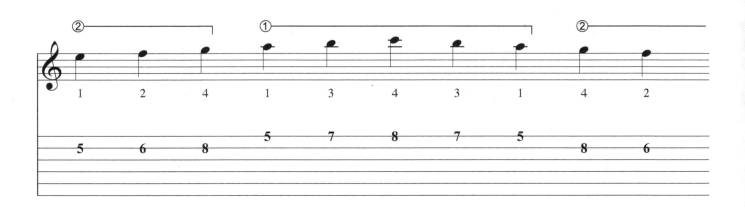

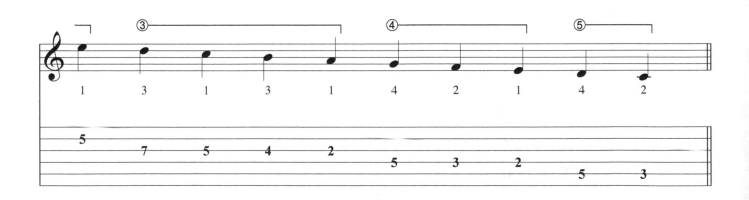

A Minor

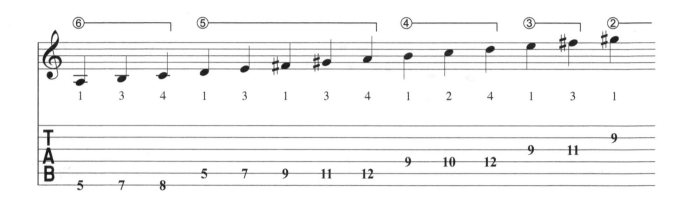

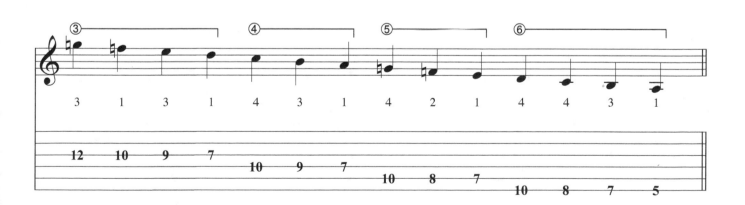

G Major

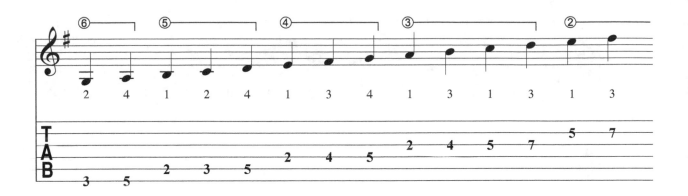

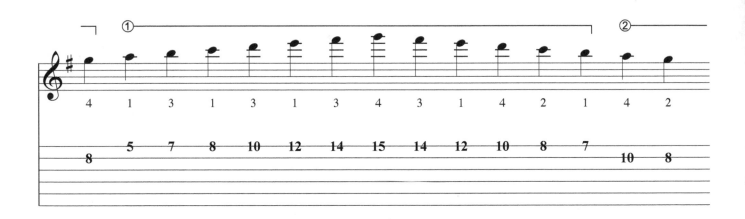

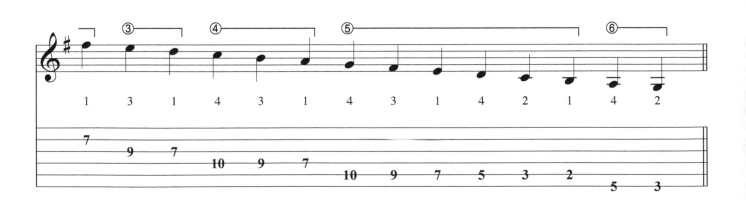

E Minor

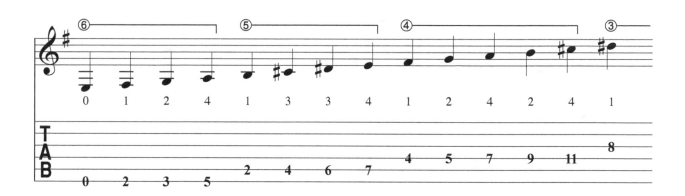

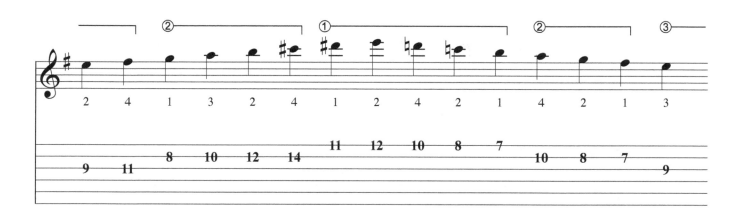

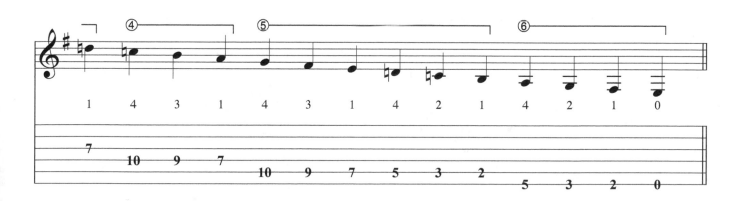

D Major

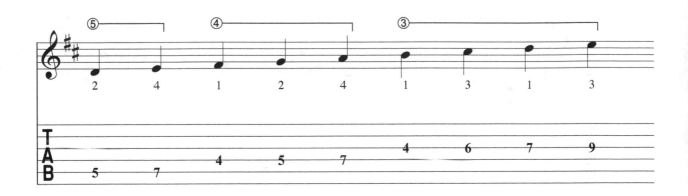

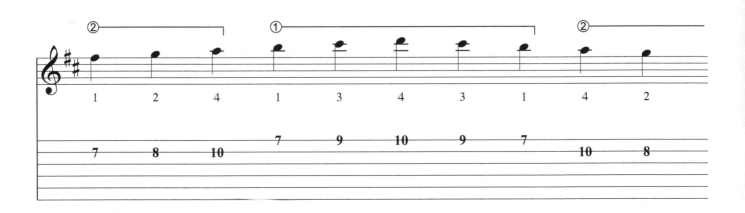

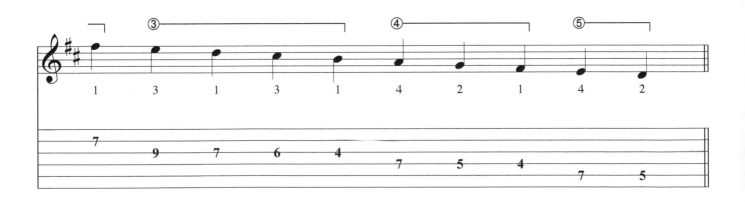

B Minor

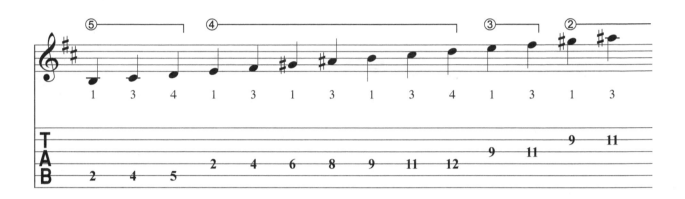

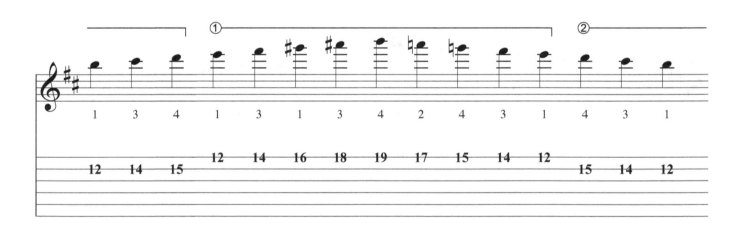

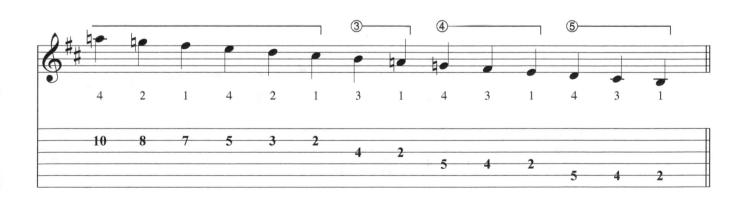

A Major

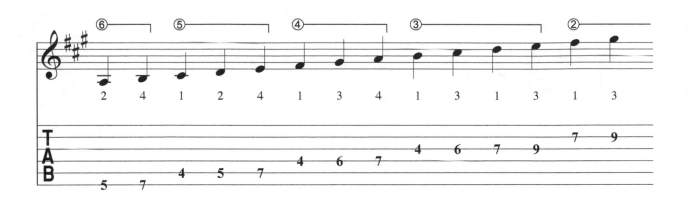

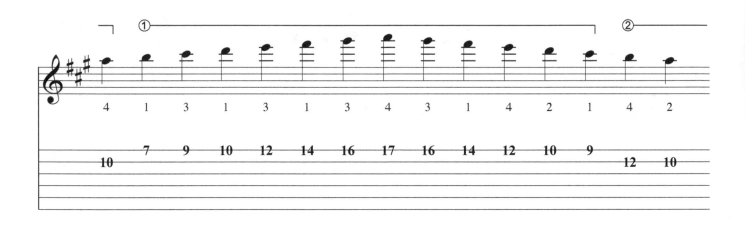

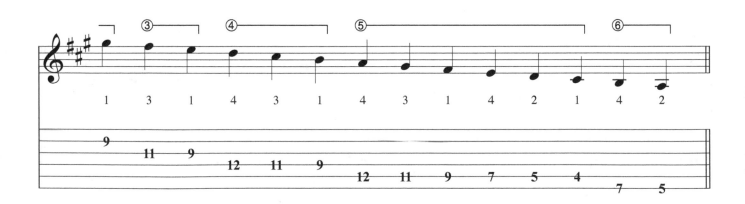

F♯ Minor

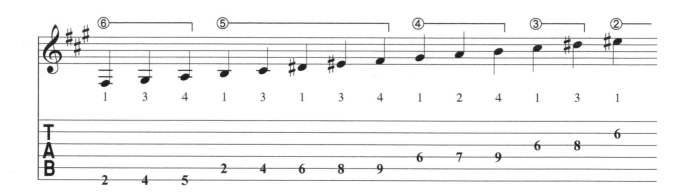

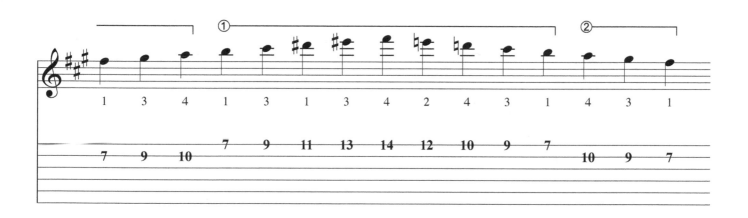

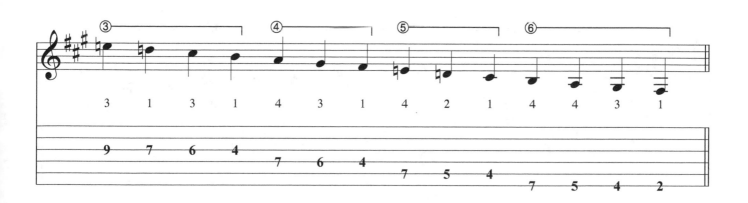

E Major

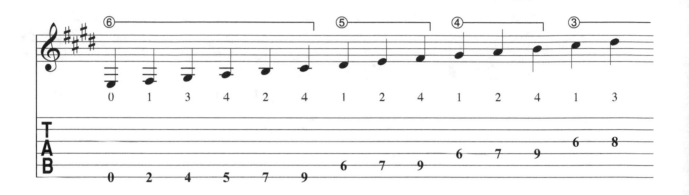

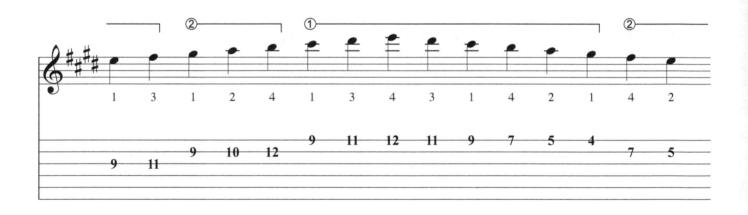

C♯ Minor

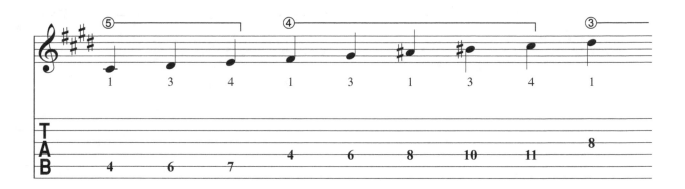

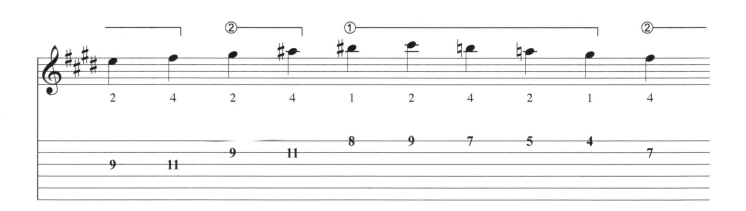

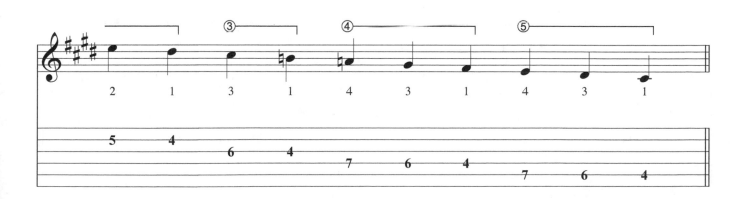

B Major

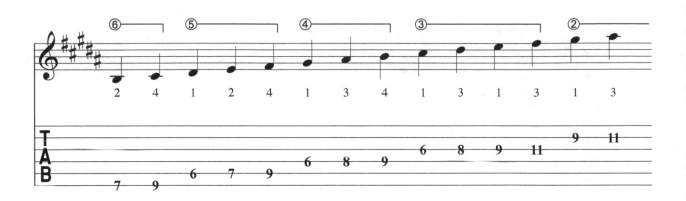

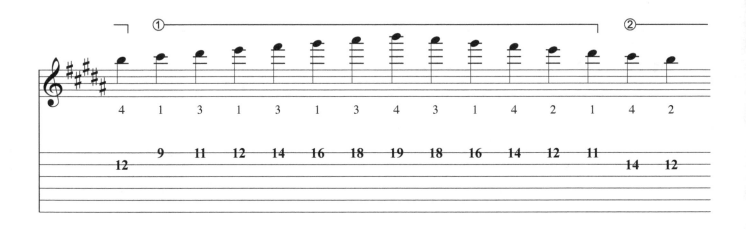

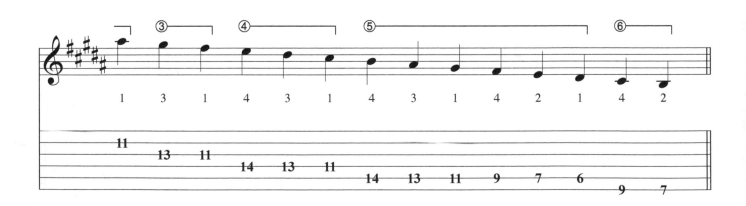

G♯ Minor

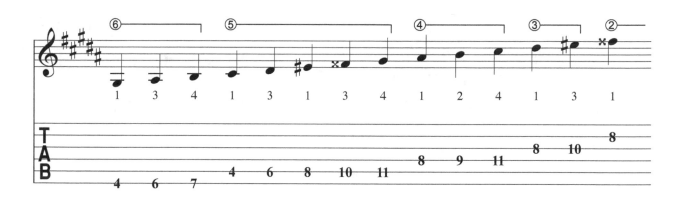

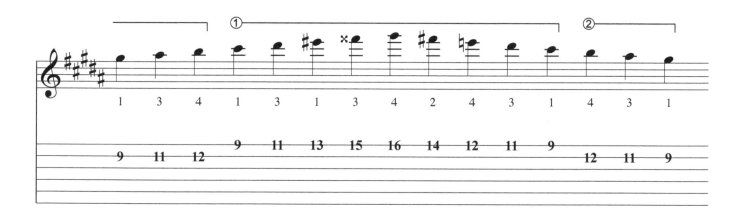

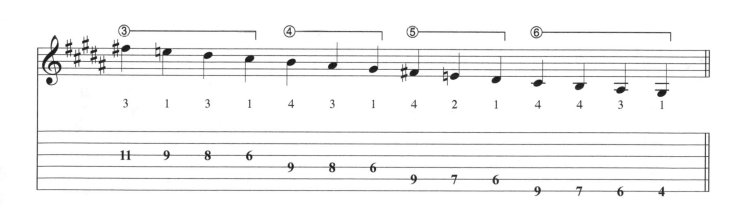

F♯ Major

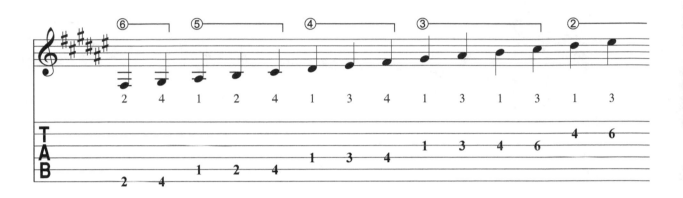

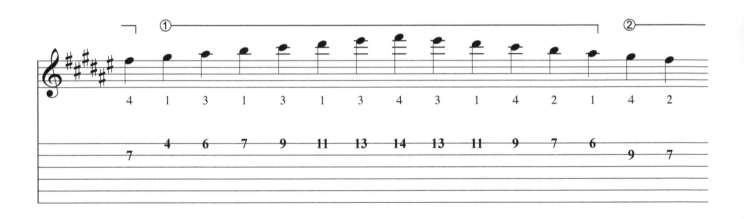

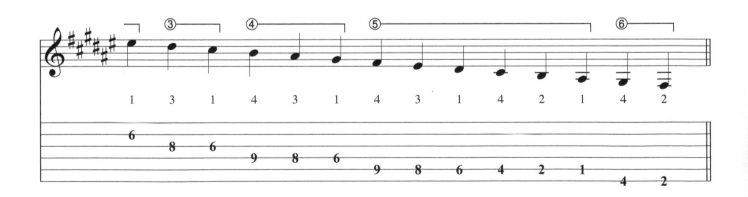

D# Minor

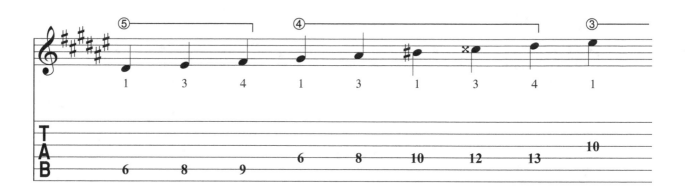

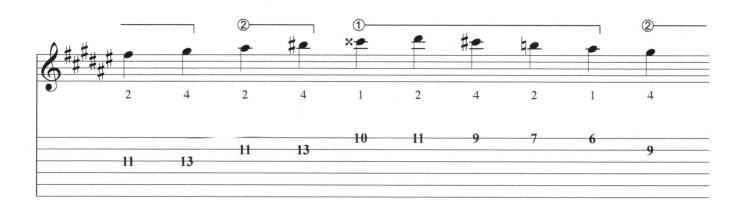

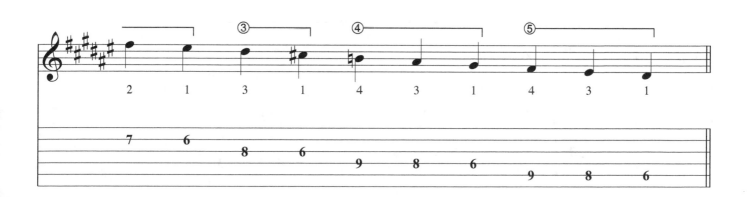

Db Major

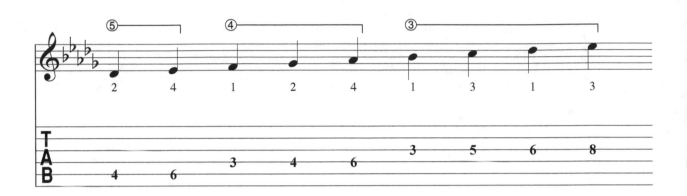

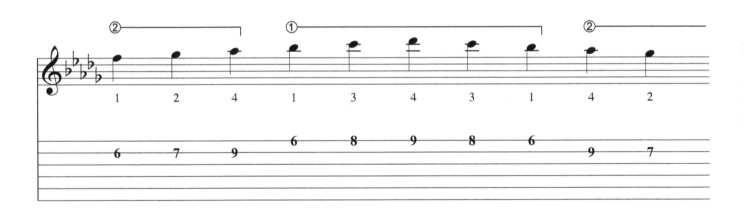

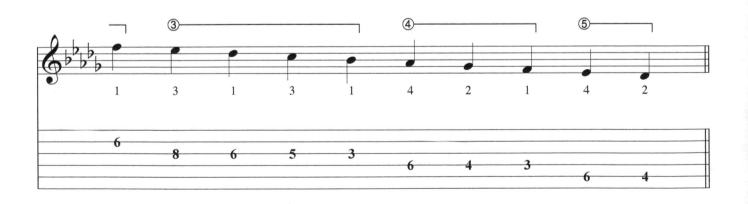

B♭ Minor

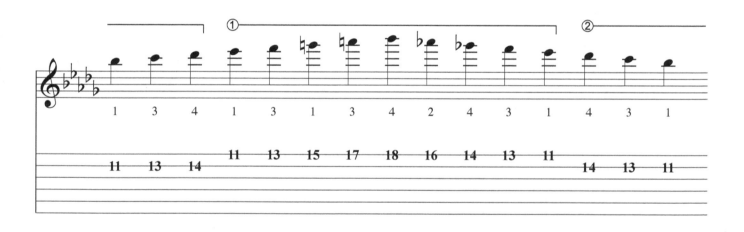

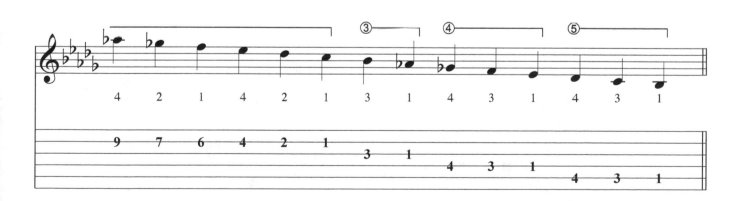

A♭ Major

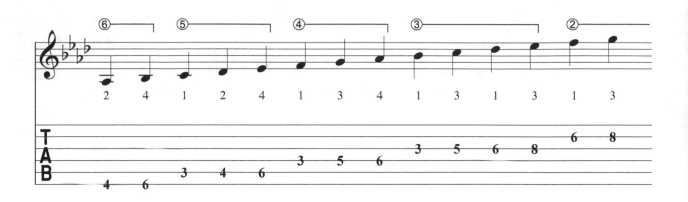

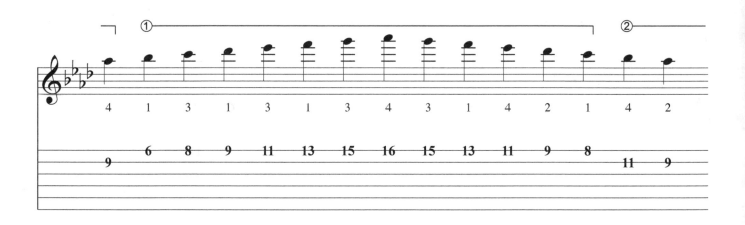

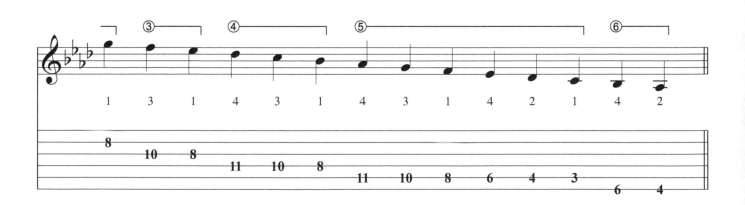

F Minor

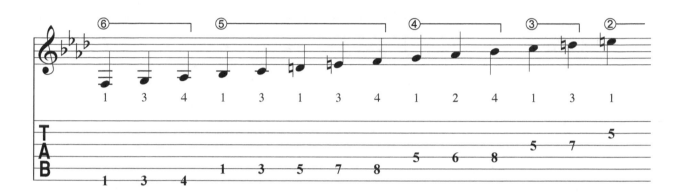

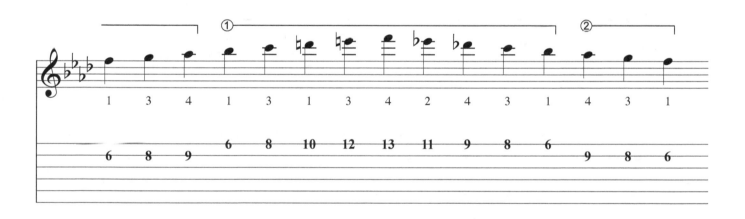

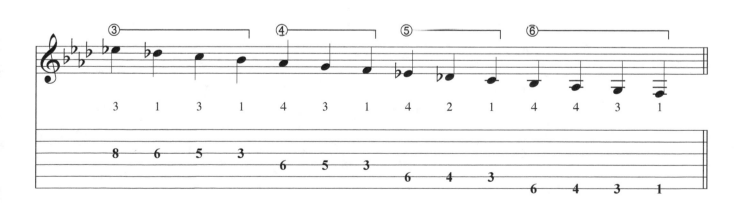

E♭ Major

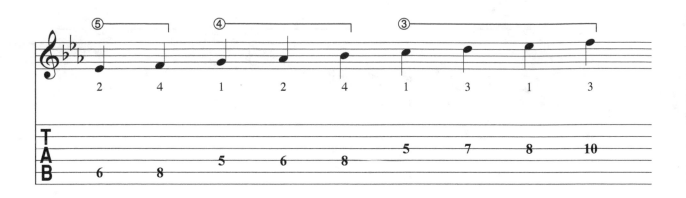

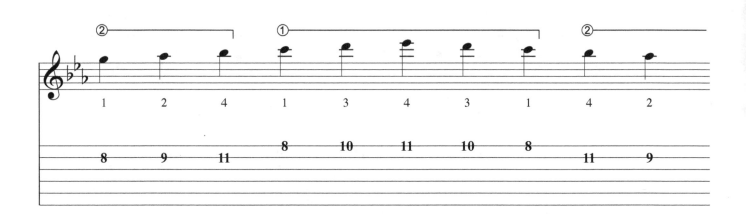

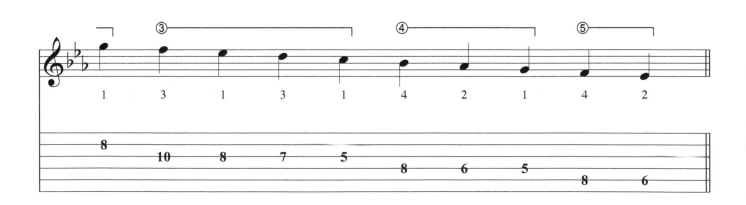

C Minor

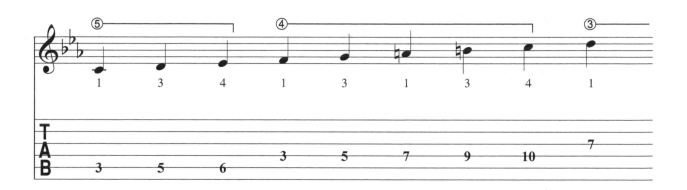

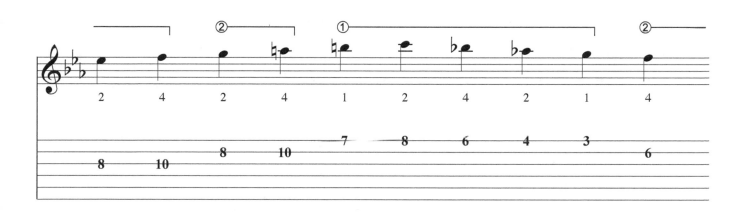

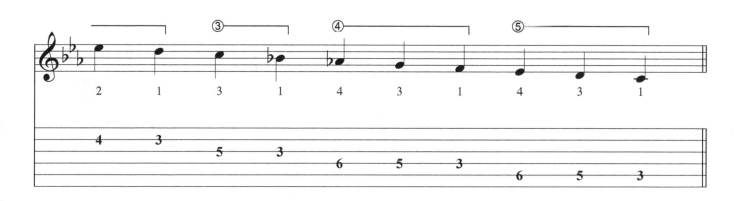

B♭ Major

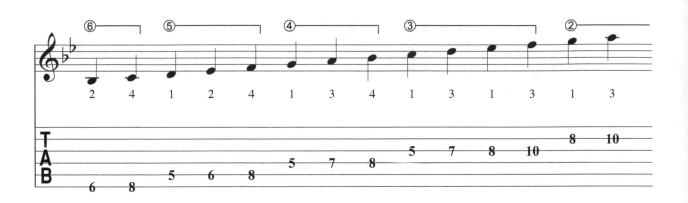

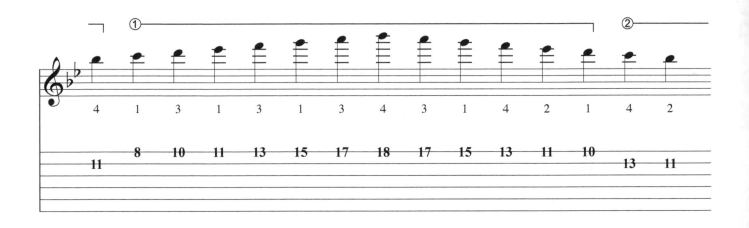

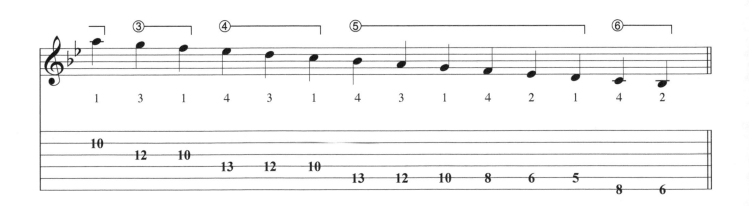

24

G Minor

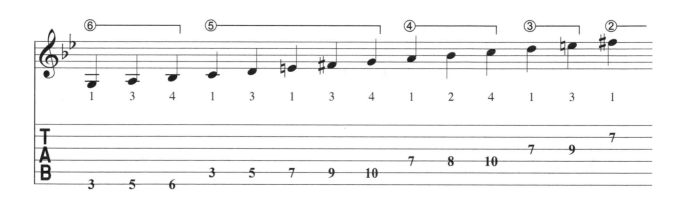

F Major

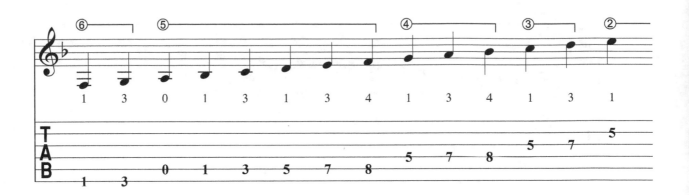

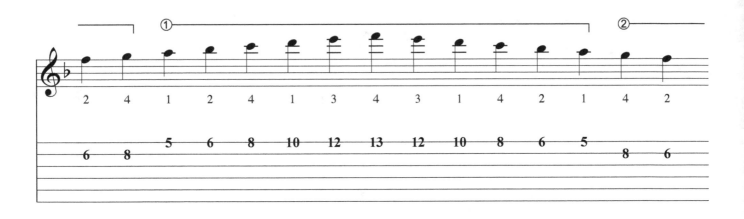

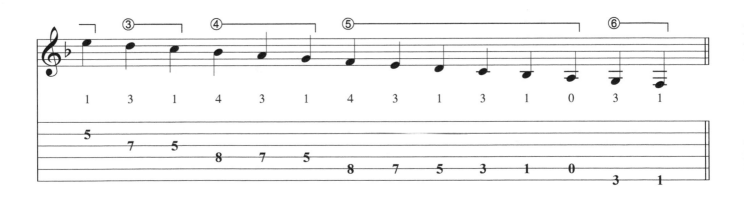

26

D Minor

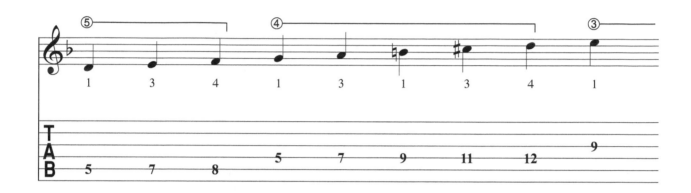

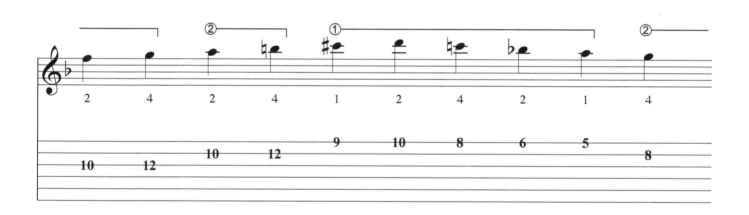

CPSIA information can be obtained
at www.ICGtesting.com
Printed in the USA
LVHW011742020123
736292LV00007B/207